CW00517388

Molehills and Coffee Spills

Poems by Harvey Aspell

Mum, this would not have been possible without your love and support.

CONTENTS

Drifting

I drifted into your eyes
With a passion
I let go, in hope things might happen

And now you're not here
I'm sparking inside
From the electricity of you

You've got me dosed
And when your lips moved close
It was only so I could hear you better

A kiss, undisclosed

Roses

I see a pretty girl at the window
A whistle wouldn't do it from here
She's neatly wrapping herself into a scarf
Rosy cheeks
Upon a rounded smile
And I think to myself
Is she just leaving?
For her roses will surely redden some more
In this weather

Daydreams

The baker's girl
Whisks up daydreams
Of the boy
At the riverside florist

Her eyes doughy
Lost in sweet swirls
Of rose petal cake frosting

The young florist
Hands pieces of flowering heather
To ladies passing by

Breaking in the day
He visits the local family-run bakery
For a bagel
And a warm smile

Wish

In love
With the prettiest girl in town
I wish I knew her

Blink

Every time I blink
I have tiny dreams about you
And I want so much
To keep my eyes closed
So they last longer
But it's all at risk
Of missing you in person

Space Exploration

I caught her standing in a bed of flowers
Naming constellations
Tie-dye dress amongst petals
The universe was in her eyes
I shot into space
To meet her gaze
And I moved like a star
Maybe she wished upon me?

Masterpiece

From across the square
The blue in your skirt
Met the green in my eyes
And my toes curled as you came closer
You laid down next to me
And it was like I had been kissed by the sky
The cool, city breeze swept across us
Blues and greens
Side by side like two brushes
At ease in the waters of a masterpiece

Decaf

After we had coffee, I knew
Because I was drinking decaf, yet
I felt so alive

My Universe

Sitting next to you
Is like being a spaceman
The sun
The Earth
And the stars
Never looked so good

Your Light

Do you remember?
Lying beneath a blanket of stars
Next to the pond
And the moon bright in the water?
It looked like a postcard

Well, that night
It was you that shone brightest
I laid beside you
Giggling
So happy to be in your light

With the moon and stars overhead
I'm wishing now
To be wherever you are

Angel

Can you love too hard
An angel?
Sweet like a vitamin
Beside you in the uncut grass
Against an orange setting sun
Listening to goslings
Bedding down for the night

And as light fades
You meander back
Through the canopy of trees
Loving too hard
This angel?
Skipping next to you, occasionally
To match your strides
But unaware
That it's your heart that's racing

You can love too hard
An angel

Moon Rose

Thousands of miles
But only one moon
And it's full tonight
I've imagined a rose on its surface
Can you see it?
Imagine it free from the atmosphere
Petals falling
Amongst the stars

Somewhere Beautiful

Imprints in the long grass
And the sky is ours
Still, in contentment
Fingers touching
Steady breaths
Aircraft meeting our gaze
Where are they flying to?
Somewhere beautiful, perhaps
For us, we're already there

Glow

I've felt the sun
Before it has risen
A perfect glow
In the darling hours
Waking up next to you

Button Moons

Resting my head
Gently on your stomach
I've closed my eyes
Surrendered to your button moons
Their gravity pulling so much
My heart monsoons
And I'm floating
Just the sound of my own breath
Pushing around little stars
In this make-belief galaxy
That I take myself to

Lemonade

Over cold lemonade
We gazed upon sun-soaked hills
And our thighs were touching
And our hearts were burning
And the bubbles in our tumblers
Yearning
For loving sips

Handprint

That moment when I kissed you
And moved you from the downpour
Into the lamplight
Where I swept the hair
From your eyes
And told you it will be all right
You smiled to the sky
And breathed a sigh
My handprint on your heart

Lavender and Rose

The likes of you and I
Need oceans and streams
Pink crustaceans
Moving sideways in our dreams
We need wet sand
Between our toes
A sky emblazoned
With lavender and rose

Hourglass

When we're together
I feel an hourglass flip in my chest
Because there's a sudden rush
And time feels so precious

Peppermint

There was this one time
When she came home
And her fringe was parted
Every time I spoke
She'd close down her eyes
I remember
I followed her into the kitchen
Where she stood motionless
By the kettle
And we both fell silent
She poured herself a peppermint tea
Since when did she drink it?

Whisper

Whisper it to me
Then it could pass as a dream
And if you regret what you say
It will undo at the seam
The words will fall light
Curtailed by the breeze
Broken down in flight
Scattered in the seas
Just whisper it to me
Tell it to me another day

Pillow

You look ravishing, I say
Sprawled lazily

She pouts in the mirror
Adjusts her skirt
You think I will be cold?

Rolling over to her pillow
The scent of citrus shampoo hits me
No, it's warm outside, I say

I don't want to go, she says
But I know I should

Go, I say
But I won't be coming
For I am closer to you
By this pillow

Daiquiri

You're dancing with your eyes closed
One hand slipped inside your skirt waist
Splashes of daiquiri on your top
The soles of your white trainers twisting in the disco lights
And you're making the DJ smile
His eyes search for you every time he sips from that paper cup
But the record doesn't skip
The music has got you feeling good
And you're blowing imaginary kisses
I can't tell if they're for me or not

Heartache

I've got you
But still, my heart aches
Every time you slip into your morning gown
And disappear to make tea
And I
I lay there
Pretending there's no pain
Wondering what to do

Crashed

You let out a big sigh
And pulled me to one side
You held my hand and looked through me
You had a fractured brow, restless
Then uttered the words
"I'm just not in love with you"
And your head dropped
And my heart crashed
And I woke up
Now I'm waiting to hear from you

Sailing

This feeling is incredible
And my face has fallen into a sad shape
Such loneliness
Please, somebody hold me
And show me pictures of the ocean
I'll try sailing
Things will pick up
Like the wind, right?

Spaceman

In my need for you
I'm meeting others
Stepping into their worlds
Searching for that magic
That blew my mind
And opened my heart
When our eyes first met
I'm going to be a spaceman
For a while
At least, until
You radio for me to come home

Snow

I slept to a light dusting of snow
And awoke to a white canvas
I drew a self-portrait in a car windshield
And followed my footprints back inside
I put the kettle on and shivered
As the steam danced around me
I peered down onto the street
And saw my face smiling up at me

Jasmine Kiss

Teapot steam
Against shades of green
The natural serene
A jasmine kiss
Washing the morning from his eyes
And the plants give a knowing look
While silence is enjoyed

Everyday

After breakfast he goes out to his garden
He perches on the stump
Using a cane for support
He takes a long-drawn breath
The air is fresh
The lawn flirts with him
Shimmering drops of dew
His breath clouds in the chill
He tips over a small terracotta pot with his cane
Spilling oats
And soon a robin lands
He keeps as still as he can
While the robin has its breakfast

After lunch he slides open his French doors
He squints into the midday sun
He sighs at the crack in his shed window
A fox scurries across the end of the garden
He doesn't see it
The sky rumbles as a plane passes over
And a light breeze picks up
Whisking a dandelion into the house
He turns to see it touching down on the carpet

After dinner he pulls back the curtain
He presses his nose against the glass
Forming a patch of mist
The volume on radio is booming
Discussions on the future of public libraries
He opens the door ajar
The cold air blows against his ankles
His security light comes on
And he watches a spider startled on its web

After breakfast he goes out to his garden
He perches on the stump
Using a cane for support
Everything is shrouded in a thick blanket of fog

Older

When she smiled at the older man
For her, that's all it was
But for him, well
It knocked him sideways
He turned his head in embarrassment
Only to catch himself
Reflecting in the window
His wrinkles looked glaringly obvious
And in the reflection, he too saw
The woman getting up to leave

Evelyn's Park

In that moment
It was Evelyn's park
The birds, the rustle in the trees, the distant church bell
Carrying her
And if she closed her eyes
She could feel Harold at her side
Their Sunday morning walk again

Blind

He's sat opposite me
His head is tilted
Every passenger is staring
At those white eyes
Drawn together by a frown
"this train terminates here"
We rush for the doors
And his fingers rush around the cane

Jellied Eels

No, no, no, lad, you're doing it all wrong
Ladies first, that's basics that is
Oh dear, she would have liked her chair pulled there
Take...her...coat, too late
Ah, but there you go, opening her menu, nice touch
It's not over yet
Now, keep eye contact
At least look engaged, lad
Betty didn't like me switching off
Good, that's good
She's looking relaxed
And she's a pretty little thing too
You might want to hold onto this one
Oh, where are you off to?
The gents? Already?
She'll think you're the shy type...

Okay, swiftly done
I'll let you off there, lad
When nature calls...
Now, she adjusted her lipstick when you were gone
A good sign that
Oh, very nice, a gentle touch on her shoulder
And she's smiling too
Take a bow, lad
Let her order first
And you order sensibly now
Betty couldn't look at me when I had the jellied eels

Sparkling

Lights catch in the silk lapels
As he sways between tables
Cigar smoke in tow
Bow tie hung loosely at his neck
Shirt escaping his fly
Microphone pressed to his lips
Beads of sweat gathering
At his weathered brow
A black thumbnail
Liver spots
Eyes, sparkling

Top Deck

I'm on the top deck of this bus
And a young lad
Sticks his arm out
From under the shelter
Well, this bus
It stops to let him on
He's a chubby little fella
Shoelaces untied
Big nostrils
Has a fluffy top lip type thing
Trying to grow one
And he's having a go on a ciggie
So, buses being non-smoking and all that
He does the decent thing
Takes a long drag before 'opping on
And flicks the dog-end to the kerb
I can smell it at this point
The smoke has come up
Through the little window
Setting off the old dear in front of me
Well, this lad
He emerges top deck
And slumps directly behind me
I knew he would
And he's panting away
The steps took it out of him, like
So, the bus moves on
I'm sitting there
Minding my own business
And now all I can feel
Are his smoky breaths
Coming and going at my ear
Well, you'll never guess what I did...

Brushes

A long road
Stretched through a tunnel
All is black and white
Particles of dust in the air
A motorbike turned on its side
And out floats a butterfly
Bright green
Two of them, in fact
The artist
Clumsy with his brushes

Ticker Tape

Ticker tape in my mind
Answers hard to find
Now the floor needs sweeping
And my eyes need sleeping
But even then
The world doesn't stop turning
And more tape falls
Forming a bed of hysteria

Leather

Me as I should have been
Is buying a car today
My bones just shook
Now I'm signing the registration book
Fresh leather interior smell
I can tell
But when I open my eyes
It's the leather bag
Of the passenger next to me
On the train

Daddy

Will I ever be called "Daddy"?
Hold a tiny hand in mine
Get to say "just like your Mother"
Have Grandparents on the line

Will I be looked up to?
And asked questions why
Make exciting promises
Be woken by a cry?

Little Brother

I've watched his cotton wool blue eyes turn to steel
And he casts a taller shadow now
With young life upon his shoulders
Still my little brother though

Marbles

They did it again
They turned their back on me
Last time they did this
I ran away
I had marbles in my pocket
And I threw them at trees
But this time
I'm just going to stand here
And when they turn back around
They can think about
Why they even invited me

Sweet Wrappers

They all throw their sweet wrappers into the stream
Every lunchtime
It's not particularly nice
But then some schoolboys are guilty of much worse

It was a Friday
And the boys were on their usual lunch walk through the woods
They were a little rowdier than normal
With the weekend coming up
Each chomping on candy bars and downing sherbet from tubes

Curtis was walking ahead of the group
He was making fun of the way their Maths teacher walks
The boys were laughing and egging him on
That is until he peeled his sticky sweet wrapper from his fingers
And flicked it into the stream

He turned to find the other boys charging at him
And thwack! He's landed flat on his back in the shallow water
Looking up he could see the treetops swaying against a grey sky
And hear the boys running away

Lunchtime on Monday
Curtis hangs back in the group
Jacket zipped up to his chin
Hands fixed inside the pockets
And his heart thumps in his chest
As they approach the stream

He didn't buy sweets today
Thought it would draw attention to Friday's incident
And he didn't want a repeat of that
Instead with tears in his eyes
He follows the group past the stream
Clutching an apple his Mum packed for him
Inside one of those pockets

Secret

And his secret
Whispered to me at a pay phone
Explained why he was so aloof
So I never made that call

Wild Blood

Chances of sleep
Long gone
My heart bangs
Like a gong
And it's deafening
I toss and turn
Prickly
Hotspots on my skin
Pulsating
Wild blood tonight

Shooting Stars

She's not shy, is she?
The moon
Blowing kisses at the sun
Shooting stars
That's what they are, you know
It's why the sun blushes in the evening
People down here wish upon those stars
But up there
It's just romance

Cynthia

The kettle whistles and trembles on the stove
And when the steam clears
I notice our housemaid
Kneeling in the garden next to the wash tub
Sunlight is playing with her auburn hair
And a tiny bird is standing in her shadow
Braving the splashes

I gently press the window open
And I can hear her humming
She's on her feet now
Clutching a white bedsheet
Twirling with it
Dipping from view, behind trees
With smiley eyes

For a moment
I fooled myself
That she was Cynthia

Concourse

I was walking behind a young couple the other day
And we approached an escalator
I noticed him gently place his hand on her lower back as they
stepped on

I smiled to myself and breathed a sigh
I dropped my gaze
And stared at the metal grooves beneath my feet

When we reached the top of the escalator
I was fine
I smiled and breathed another sigh
So much sunshine was pouring onto the concourse

Timeless Moment

The back of her watch strap
Has captured her scent
A sweetness released
Her presence lent
With the numbers turned
Curiosity has earned
A timeless moment
With her

Pancakes

Stood at the hob
A dab of butter in the pan
Smooth whispers
And I'm thinking about your arms around my waist
A feeling so well accompanied with the heat
Your lips gently pressed against the nape of my neck
And your hand, grabbing my tummy
"Yes, yes, I know..." I needn't say it though
You've heard it all before
But that kiss...
It takes over
Like the butter
Melting on the steel
A sensual touch
Of you I still feel

Jukebox

I will never forget the way
Our hips would swing and sway
Down at Eddie's Ballroom
Your curls bouncing on your shoulders
And Timmy watching on, red in the face
Sleeves always rolled up past his elbows
You kissed me hard one evening
Tell me, did you fix the dent in your Chevy?
I remember the blinkers reflecting in puddles
And my denim pants getting soaked on the hood

I pass Eddie's on the freeway from time to time
Thoughts of you dancing to Tutti Frutti
Come rushing back
Frantic polka dots on the dance floor
And it's funny, I always glance in the rear-view mirror
Because you liked sitting in the back, remember?
Legs stretched out between the two front seats
The acoustic guitar in hand, mind you
So I was fine with that
My car radio never worked anyway
Perhaps that's why we hogged the jukebox?

Black Paint

You pried open a tin of black paint
We never used black
And with my hands tied
You engulfed our canvas
You chose the colour
Of your heart

Grey

Forgive me
For all the grey
But at times
When the sun and rain collide
The colours are just too much
And grey
Is the colour of stone
For support
You see

Earring

You've got my tears
You've got my laughter
You've got my secrets
You've got my pride
You've got my love
You've got my heart
I've got your earring
Found it in the hallway

Bluebird

Hey there little bluebird
Who plucked you from the sky?
What's that?
She wants to see me?
Okay, but I'm fall hard every time that happens
Why don't you fly back to her, and say
"He wants to feel you"
Because I want so much more than visits
What was that?
She's scared?
I don't know why, bluebird
Are you peckish, by the way?
Here, have some seed
It keeps your blue bright
You see, if I had wings like you
I'd take her by the hand and fly away
To a place where she'd be free of worry
And we'd fall into each other
Say what?
A dreamer?
I am a dreamer, yes
Don't you ever wish you had fingers?
To run through a woman's hair?
See, we all dream
That's your flock, look
Go, be with them and enjoy the flight
I'll sit tight
And maybe she'll fly to me

Soon

I've been thieving
I stole the speckles from the moon
A brighter illumination now
Maybe I'll find you soon

Three Years

When I stepped on the tube
It was then
I saw her
And I still adored her
My heart was shaking
Not from the carriages on the tracks
But little love attacks
I could breathe her in once more
Her long blue coat
Touching the floor
Just feet away
And what did I say?
Nothing today
She smiled into her book
A new, content look
I just took her all in
Didn't know where to begin
Her eyes so dreamy
Lips so full
I could taste the gin
That she drunk on the night
When it felt floaty and light
The same bracelet as now
Seems three years did allow
One more moment with her
The station approached
And she breathed a sigh
I didn't say hello
And I didn't say goodbye

Latte

You'd barely arrived at the table
And there I went
The shape of your lips
Full, so full of love
Soft to touch still, I imagine
And that little crease in your nose
Probably from where you've smiled so often
A new ring, I noticed
Copper, is it? Or bronze
Regardless, you wear it well
Your gaze still drifts
During conversation
And I never minded that
I like wondering where you go
Well, the latte was pretty average
But it was the best coffee I've had in years

Molehills and Coffee Spills

We don't spend enough time out here
Walk with me
Link your arm with mine
Careful, your coffee is spilling
Isn't it wonderful?
We can walk these grounds without being disturbed
You know that, don't you?
It's private
I own it all
You could go for some nice runs around here
Between the ferns
Over the brook
Of course, I'll be timekeeping
My knees aren't up to it now
That's a beautiful smile
I am a lucky man
Come closer
You feel so distant sometimes
There you go
That's how it should be
Look at those
Molehills
That's what they are
You'll have to be careful
Your ankles, I mean
When you go running

Star

Just a star
In the distance
Shining brightly
For somebody

Printed in Great Britain
by Amazon

61233133R00043